T0348862

FOR NOW I AM SITTING HERE GROWING TRANSPARENT

愈坐愈透明

Selected Poems *of* YAU CHING

游靜

Translated from Chinese by

Chenxin Jiang 江晨欣

Zephyr Press

Cover photograph by Yau Ching
Book design by typeslowly
Printed in Michigan by Cushing Malloy

The Hong Kong Atlas is a series of contemporary Hong Kong writing in English
translation. Established with funds from the Hong Kong Arts Development Council,
titles include poetry, prose, and graphic adaptations from established and emerging
Hong Kong authors.

We acknowledge with gratitude the financial and administrative support
of the Hong Kong Arts Development Council, the Massachusetts Cultural Council,
and The Academy of American Poets with funds from the
Amazon Literary Partnership Poetry Fund.

The Hong Kong Arts Development Council fully supports freedom of artistic expression.
The views and opinions expressed in this project do not represent the stand of the Council.

Cataloging-in-publication data is available from the Library of Congress.

ISBN 978-1938890345

CONTENTS

PROSE POEMS 散文詩

DEATH AND ADVENTURE 亡命與半途

Yau Ching's Self-Translating Poems

Written in Cantonese-inflected standard Chinese, Yau Ching's poems are simultaneously erudite and earthy, shaped by Hong Kong's cultural position on the margins of mainland China and at the center of the Cantonese-speaking world. Her oeuvre spans gender, aesthetics, and colonial politics, encompassing a vast range of registers. It includes astute political poems, understated love poems, urban anti-eclogues, and meandering prose poems.

Born in Hong Kong in 1966, Yau Ching studied media studies in New York and London. She then spent many years teaching in Hong Kong and Taipei, while also founding and programming several film festivals dedicated to the stories of sex workers and the queer community. Her parallel lives as an award-winning video artist and queer community organizer are evident in the crisp imagery and socially radical outlook that characterize her work. The poems in this collection are arranged in four sections: "Home" (on the shifting site of Hong Kong), "You" (in which the poetic voice is often addressed to a female lover/listener), "Prose Poems," and "Death and Adventure" (themes central to Yau Ching's work).

With millions joining street protests in 2019, a draconian security law passed in 2020, and countless pro-democracy activists arrested since then, Hong Kong has made headlines in recent years. But long before the city's current political struggles, Yau Ching was writing with startling prescience about the impossibility of Hong Kong's position caught between Britain and China. Having witnessed Hong Kong's entrepôt trade-and-manufacturing-fuelled boom, Yau Ching is clear-eyed about the city's vulnerability.

In "You and Us," one of the poems in the section "Home," Yau Ching compares Hong Kong's position to that of a pawn in a game of chess played by Britain and China:

> We're the letter-bearing
> Rosencrantz and Guildenstern
> when the letter is opened our heads will be chopped
> off and this letter this letter
> is called democracy

In Yau Ching's reading of Hong Kong history, the elusive goal of democracy is a double-edged sword, comparable to the letter Rosencrantz and Guildenstern carry. Her poetic skepticism recalls the revelations (by Jonathan Dimbleby among others) that UK officials privately undermined their public commitment to a democratic Hong Kong in discussions with their Chinese counterparts. The mere invocation of democracy is more betrayal than promise. As Yau Ching points out in "You and Us," Hong Kongers have never had the right to self-determination codified in international law and granted to so many other peoples, the option of turning their home into a "home/land" (a word that coincidentally and felicitously mirrors the Chinese "國/家" in this poem), a sovereign state.

In "No City," Yau Ching takes on what is arguably Hong Kong's most defining physical and economic reality, its high population density and cost of housing. Home is a fraught concept in a city peopled by refugees and the children of refugees, where "no one remains" and "no flats remain" because of the cost of housing.[1] Like Yau Ching's other political

---

1. In 2021, the Urban Reform Institute's Demographia International Housing Affordability Study ranked Hong Kong the world's most expensive property market. The market has softened since the COVID-19 pandemic but still makes Hong Kong one of the least affordable international cities.

poems, "No City" does not reference current events; rather, her work grapples with the underlying economic and historical causes of the city's postcolonial predicament.

Yau Ching's description of Hong Kong as an island in "Island Country" is not geographically literal, since the city also encompasses a peninsula; it is, however, a poignant image for what her poems read as the city's simultaneous insularity and openness. For much of the city's colonial history, English was its only official language. Chinese gained official, albeit secondary status in 1974; the vast majority of Hong Kongers, however, speak Cantonese as their main language (89% of the city's residents according to the 2021 census).[2] While Hong Kong used to have many languages, Yau Ching writes, they've since crystallized into the two official languages, English and Chinese:

> There's an island
> that used to have many languages, now they've become
> one called English   another Chinese . . .
> if your name is not an English name
> the island will give you one

Such a pronouncement underscores the speaker's insistence that standard Chinese is not her own language—and indeed, the Cantonese

---

2. A brief, imprecise primer: Hong Kong's Chinese speakers mostly speak the southern Chinese language of Cantonese, and read and write standard Chinese, the lingua franca invented by early 20th-century reformers and based on Mandarin, the language of much of northern China. While a given sentence in standard Chinese can be read aloud with Cantonese phonology, it generally differs in vocabulary and grammatical structure from the same sentence in Cantonese. Yau Ching's poems are mostly written in what I refer to as "Cantonese-inflected standard Chinese," standard Chinese with some word choices influenced by Cantonese. For more on Cantonese, I suggest Victor Mair's posts on the blog Language Log.

inflection in lines such as "no one can leave" (所有人都沒得走) makes her point. In "The Temptations of Eden," Yau Ching bluntly asserts: "We are orphans / who don't belong in Asia." The Hong Kong she describes is a "ruined city" whose isolation stems from the fact that it has never fit in with its surroundings, a metaphorical island that comprises a collection of physical islands.

In another poem, "Hong Kong Malady," the speaker describes life in "the box called Hong Kong" as she physically experienced it, through the chronic headaches and breathing difficulties she had as a child, which persisted until she grew up and left the city. Health, the speaker says, is "just numbness" to the world. To the extent that writing is the antithesis of that numbness, poetry itself is the speaker's "Hong Kong Malady."

Very few writers of Yau Ching's generation of Hong Kong poets are openly queer, making her perspective a singular one. The poems in the second section, "You," often posit a dialogue between a female speaker and a female listener (妳) to whom the poem is addressed. These poems brim with the mundane details of everyday urban life: the speaker takes the subway, dreams of a dim sum restaurant, and frequently invokes her cat, even while allusions to multiple languages and cities indicate a cosmopolitan backdrop.

Yau Ching's work establishes intimacy with its deep attunement to language. Many of the poems in this section ("Distance," for instance, or "Embrace") use short lines to make space for silence within the poem itself:

> Keep
> a little distance
> to make
> the heart grow fonder

In them, wordplay is a form of intimacy. The poem "Moon" invokes the traditional Chinese equivalence between the full moon and familial togetherness, while creating its own associations between time, space, and the beloved's name:

> Mona,
> I almost forgot to say
> our *month*
> also means *moon*

Yau Ching was unusual in being open about her attraction to women from the early 1990s onwards, and her poems subtly gesture at a politics of queerness that was even more marginal in Hong Kong at the time of writing than it is now. Nor do her love poems shy away from asking political questions. In "Always," the listener is a (female) "you" with whom the speaker contemplates rows of female store clerks bowing outside a Japanese department store, asking her listener how the store clerks feel about this display of feminine submission:

> not a crease in a stocking not that these women
> had a choice   or would they always be inclining in our direction

While the female coding of the listener cannot be succinctly captured in translation, since English does not have gendered second-person pronouns, the shared gender of speaker, listener, as well as the store clerks only intensifies the urgency of the speaker's rhetorical question.

The poems in "Prose Poems" are thematically and stylistically wide-ranging: a veiled reference to the Tiananmen Square protests, an account of taking the ferry in Hong Kong, and vignettes of student life in San Francisco. What ties them together is the form of the prose poem, which in Yau Ching's case, is closely tied to the freewheeling nonfiction prose form known as saan²man⁴ 散文, as well as the culture of fu³hon¹ 副刊, the literary supplements to daily newspapers. (It is unprofitable here to pursue the definitional question of where prose poems end and saan^{2}man^4 begin—suffice it to say that Yau Ching's prose always has poetic qualities and vice versa.) Yau Ching freelanced in the 1980s as a fu^{3}hon^1 columnist for *Singtao Daily* as well as the now-defunct *Express*. "I only ever write on assignment/my life is ten cents per word no pay no words," she writes in "A serialized poem for a four-hundred-and-ninety-five-word newspaper column," poking fun at the fu^{3}hon^1 columnist's need to make a living while pursuing her literary aspirations and earning the "right to call [herself] an Author."

Like the best fu^{3}hon^1 columns, Yau Ching's prose poems directly address the reader and assume her interest in the most mundane details of the speaker's life. The speaker of "Bauhaus Exercise in Vulgarization" is trying to work out what lighting to install in her room and braising chicken wings in the microwave; the speaker of "Shanghai Noodles Grow Up" is craving noodles and has just lost a phone number she wrote down. While these poems are chatty and expansive, a stylistic counterpoint to the rest of the collection, they also offer an accretion of cryptic details: a single earring, a classroom walkout, a pile of newspaper cuttings, which together offer a shrewd portrait of Hong Kong in the 1980s.

The poems in "Death and Adventure," on the other hand, operate by ellipsis. Several belong to a series of poems that Yau Ching wrote after going through chemotherapy and surgery for Stage 3 breast cancer. Others date to Yau Ching's time in the US. The final poem in the section, "Dissolve into Wind," juxtaposes a traveller and a monk, musing on the loneliness and exhaustion that, according to the poem, characterize death. It ends:

> there's something that
> while being completed
> can't be improved accumulated
> inherited revisited
>
> it's no wonder history is so

History, like death, can't help its own finality.

Poems from the bilingual collection *The Impossible Home* exist in English versions as well as Chinese ones written by Yau Ching; when beginning this collaboration, we agreed that I would also translate those since the English versions were not envisioned strictly as translations. Yau Ching's English translations often improvise on the Chinese. The poem whose title I translate as "Turning a Leaf," for instance, Yau Ching titles "Twist and Turn" in English. The title "Turning a Leaf" imperfectly captures the Chinese 轉頁 for the notion of "turning a page/turning a leaf over": in Chinese, the word for "page" is a homonym for "leaf," whereas leaf in English has echoes of "leafing through pages." Yau Ching's title, on the other hand, doubles the verb while eliding the noun, accentuating the speaker's insomniac twisting and turning ("I lie in bed imagining you turning"). Here is my translation of the end of the third stanza:

> crisp and unfalling
> like fish and chips

Yau Ching's version reads:

> crispy but not to fall (if I insist)
> like fish and chips

Missing from the poem's Chinese version, the clause "(if I insist)" adds a note of authorial doubt.

One aspect of Yau Ching's poetry that's particularly challenging to translate is its wordplay and playfulness with form. In "Invisible Man," for instance, Yau Ching splits Chinese words across two lines, evoking their separate meanings: I do the same with words such as "aim/less" and "fool/scap." "No City" is a poem composed almost entirely of six-character lines in the Chinese: just one syllable shorter than the seven-character lines standard in traditional poetry (and one longer than the five-character lines that are equally traditional). These six-character lines sound abbreviated, pressed for time, perhaps even short on space like the Hong Kong described in the poem. I attempt to capture the poem's metrical regularity in a largely dactylic translation:

> Whenever I visit a city
> I think about buying a flat
> Whenever I go to a new place
> I think about settling down

Throughout the poem, the lines grow shorter; in my translation, two rhyming five-character lines become

> impossible that
> impossible flat

By the end of the poem, lines of two or three characters mirror the speaker's insistence that ordinary residents are disappearing, being squeezed out of Hong Kong by the city's housing crisis:

> that makes us
> no body
> if not a body
> then just a no

"Trial Run," which Yau Ching notes that she wrote after a breast cancer diagnosis, is a poem that consists of that which is absent—the word "death," in lines such as

> nothing is certain but   and taxes
>   mask   knell   grip
>   blow   metal   rattle

Her poem deftly makes use of the fact that Cantonese sayings invoking death are often more whimsical than grim, an insight mirrored here with English proverbs and euphemisms for death.

Yau Ching's interlingual puns, stemming from English and found in her Chinese poems, return to English via these translations. In "Spacetime," she writes:

> Time is like a shadow on the road
> The English word longing has length in it
> I long—— long——— for you

The obscurity in Chinese of these interlingual puns is paralleled, for English readers, by the opacity of Yau Ching's Chinese-language puns. In the same poem, she writes: "Loneliness in Chinese is empty." The characters for loneliness and emptiness in Chinese share the same radical 宀, which denotes "roof." The "length" of the word longing is immediately apparent to a English reader, echoing the way in which the resonance between loneliness and emptiness is visually apparent for a Chinese one.

Since many of Yau Ching's poems draw on Cantonese words and phrases, they have a colloquial edge that forms a counterpoint to the poet's lightly worn erudition. In "Potted Plants and Path," the speaker gushes: "你就好啦," a phrase I translate as "Aren't you the lucky one," which doesn't quite capture the note of envy in the Chinese. In "Turning a Leaf," Yau Ching asks: "Doesn't *brave* rhyme with *love*," choosing two characters (敢 and 心) that rhyme in Cantonese but not in Mandarin. While Yau Ching rarely uses Cantonese characters per se, the Cantonese inflection of her poetry comes through in expressions such as 搬屋 (for moving house, in "Bauhaus Exercise in Vulgarization") or 拆樓 (for demolishing a building, in "Ask the Words") which both represent Cantonese diction while happening to use standard Chinese characters. On the other hand, English is just as likely to appear in these poems as the language of bureaucracy and of neoliberal work habits (as with "debrief" and "follow-up" in "Dissolve into Wind" or the "memo" in "Shanghai Noodles Grow Up"), as it is to invoke foreign art and artifacts (a Lomo camera, a Filofax, the name of a film).

The poet's lightly worn erudition leaves its mark. The prose poem "Ask the Words" offers an impression of San Francisco as refracted through the City Lights bookstore, in which "Frank O'Hara's plays are prominently displayed. Byron is/on sale." In "Potted Plants and Path," the speaker suggests "eating *zosui* with Ozu/and drinking Oshima under the table," balancing out allusions to films by Godard and Truffaut with oblique references to Japanese cinema. Hong Kong culture is central to Yau Ching's work, and lines quoted from Albert Leung's quintessential Cantopop lyrics (such as Leslie Cheung's "A Man of Intention," a line of which opens the poem "That's How We Met") evoke the city's dominance of Sinophone popular culture for several generations of listeners.

Yau Ching's deep knowledge of many global cities—from Tokyo to San Francisco—also finds its way into her poetry. Agnes Lam suggests defining Hong Kong poetry as that written by "poets based in Hong Kong, geographically or psychologically," the adverbial qualifiers recognizing that Hong Kong, of all places, is too porous (and perhaps just too small) to be defined by its mere physical footprint.[3] With what she calls an "unprofessional" teaching career that has thus far spanned three continents, Yau Ching is a prime example of a poet with a fluid relationship to her Hong Kong base.

Almost all of the poems collected here appear in Yau Ching's collections, *Stripping Skirts and Trousers* (1999), *The Impossible Home* (2000), *Big Hairy Egg* (2011), and *Pre-historic Documents* (2021). Many of them date to the colonial, pre-handover city. A handful of them were revised in

---

3. Agnes Lam, "Poetry in Hong Kong: The 1990s," *World Literature Today* 73.1 (1999), 59.

2020–2021 for *Pre-historic Documents.* "Bauhaus Exercise in Vulgarization" has been included in both its versions, the revised version preserving the original narrative arc—but fiercer, terser. Throughout this time, Yau Ching was also active as a video artist; in fact, as she told the Taiwanese journal *Film Appreciation,* she originally left Hong Kong for postgraduate work in the US and UK because she thought the West would be a better place to study film.[4]

As a student at the University of Hong Kong, Yau Ching began making videos, an art form she describes as having been new to Hong Kong in the 1980s, and one she hoped would have a wider audience than poetry. Like her poetic oeuvre, Yau Ching's video art is deeply personal and political, shot using VHS and Hi-8 cameras, 8mm and 16mm film, and more recently, digital formats. Yau Ching's video art practice also incorporates translation, since most of her videos are subtitled in English or Chinese.

An award-winning early 16mm film, "Is There Anything Specific You Want Me to Tell You About?" (1991), thematizes this question. The narrator voices over in English how she thinks her parents (including a father with Parkinson's disease) would respond to her video art. "If he sees this film one day, and could not make any sense out of it, he would at least recognize this scene and may perhaps know why I made it and did not dedicate it to [my parents]," she muses. "Then why did you say all this in English?" asks a hollow, echoing voice *in Cantonese.* "These images . . ." begins the narrator, but her voice is abruptly cut off. The English line indirectly addresses Yau Ching's father as an imaginary audience ("If he sees this film . . . he would at least recognize this scene") but in a language he cannot understand. By contrast, the scenes in question are Communist propaganda films from the 1960s, which would be familiar to Hong Kongers of Yau Ching's parents' generation, and perhaps draw them into her video art even as its language eludes them.

---

4. Xie Renchang, "Xingbie nilu: Duochong renting de aodi sai butu – fang youjing," *Dianying xinshang* 22.4 (Spring 2004).

To risk stating the obvious, language offers a means of accessing a specific audience, whether the narrator's father, the Anglophone audience of this video, a Sinophone audience reading the traditional Chinese subtitles, or a prize jury in the US or in Taiwan. Both Yau Ching's video art as well as her poetry wryly address their respective forms of linguistic in-betweenness. As she writes in "Island Country,": "you're not allowed/your own language." Poetry, then, is a space in which the question of permission is irrelevant; when language that is not the speaker's own enters the poem ("go north! north! north!"), it is invalidated by the processes of quotation and parody.

This is the sense in which Yau Ching's poems are self-translating: as a product of Hong Kong, itself a translated city, Yau Ching's poems enact linguistic in-betweenness while asserting the poet's right to her own language, one that has been erased by the city. This language need not necessarily be Cantonese—on occasion, as the narrator of "Is There Anything Specific You Want Me to Tell You About?" suggests, it could be English. To translate Yau Ching's poems into English is to bring them into a space that they already uneasily inhabit; it is an extension of the work that is already taking place inside the poem itself.

As Jennifer Feeley writes, Yau Ching "uses her writing to assert plural identities, imbued with a desire for the poet, her homeland, and her poetry to all be self-autonomous."[5] Such an assertion offers a range of answers to the question implicit in Yau Ching's oeuvre: in the context of Hong Kong's predicament, what is poetry for? In "To Octavio Paz," the poet puts forward an explicitly hopeful ars poetica:

---

5. Jennifer Feeley, "Heartburn on a map called home: Yau Ching and the (im)possibility of Hong Kong poetry as Chinese poetry," *Journal of Modern Literature in Chinese* 10.1 (Summer 2010), 159.

In the space between new capitalism and fake communism
poetry slices open a real republic
emptying out a homeland for two hundred and two
thousand young people without a

home

A home—a republic, a homeland even—is what Yau Ching's poems offer the reader, a home that is full of both the silences and the sound that characterize her poems, each a space defined as much by its ellipses as by what it contains.

—Chenxin Jiang

伊甸園的誘惑

我們是孤兒
不屬於亞細亞
從沒有鄰居朋友兄弟
活着被怪獸追趕
長期缺氧
呼吸大力一點都沒命
當過去變成目前
失去被尋得
天使填滿空洞
丟我們在廢城鎖上門
讓我們互相撕殺
互相鄙視又緊抱一起
用最快的磁浮速度
發射自我於太虛
經過了千山萬水等著被鄰近地區
再一次接管

這便是伊甸園

The Temptations of Eden

We are orphans
who don't belong in Asia
neighborless friendless unbrothered
all our lives we've been chased by monsters
chronically deprived of oxygen
breathing in hard would kill us
When the past became present
when the lost was found
angels filled in the holes
threw us into the ruined city and locked the gate
so we'd hack each other to pieces
scorn and cling to each other
blast ourselves into the void
past endless mountains and rivers
at the speed of the fastest bullet train and wait
to be subjugated again
by our nearest neighbor

This, then, is Eden

香港病

頭痛是一種絕症
看醫生也不過給三天必你痛
捱到OK店買
必你痛所有產品本週九折
還有藥盒鎖匙扣送
你要不要多買多送

對空氣過份敏感就是病
自小在公共屋邨就有
頭痛發熱
鼻水眼水四肢乏力
呼吸困難
整個人被一團廁紙塞著
躺在床上作古仔不想起來
不想起來十六年

然後是對食物過敏
疴疴嘔嘔
起來都是上廁所

捱到搬離這叫香港的盒子
我的敏感自動麻木下來
健康原來是一種麻木
對世界沒有
強烈的厭惡
不需要掙扎的存在
身體原來不掙扎便快樂
懷著平和的心

Hong Kong Malady

A headache being a terminal illness
the doctor won't prescribe more than three days of Panadol
so you drag yourself to Circle K
where the pills are 10% off
and come with a free keychain
buy more get more freebies

Being sensitive to the air is a malady
child of a public housing project, I had
headaches fevers
runny nose watery eyes weak limbs
couldn't breathe
every orifice stuffed with toilet paper
I'd lie in bed concocting stories, unwilling to rise
these sixteen years

Next it was the food
I'd vomit all night
only getting up to use the toilet

When I finally fled
the box called Hong Kong
my sensitivities were deadened
health itself is just numbness
deadness to the world
the body is happy when it's not putting up a fight
when you're at ease
between daylight and darkness

在白天與黃昏之間
陽光射在紅磚上不熾烈
不特別感到活著是難

在香港
我從沒健康過
懊惱納悶的心情大量發售
難怪寫作

when the sunlit bricks aren't scorching
being alive isn't that hard

In Hong Kong
I have never been healthy
Boredom and irritation come wholesale
is it any wonder I write

島國

有這麼一個島
本來有很多語言變成
一種叫英文　一種叫中文
你任何時候都不准
用自己的話語
你的名字如果非英文
島會給你一個

有這麼一個島
整天想象自己是國
整天嚷着要有尊嚴！尊嚴！尊嚴！
愈喊愈滿腔悲憤　淚流披臉
淹沒五千年委屈
把一個電視台
砌起來哭倒長城

有這麼一個島
只有牆沒有門
所有人都沒得走於是認定了
自己是跨國集團嚷着國際！國際！國際！
只有加倍愛國才能置身國外(北上！北上！北上！)
然後嚷着羞恥！羞恥！羞恥！
愈喊愈滿腔妬恨
哀生不逢時　懷才不遇
仇富怨窮把所有俊男美女放逐
用味精燒臘盡快毒死自己

有這麼一個島

Island Country

There's an island
that used to have many languages, now they've become
one called English   another Chinese
you're not allowed
your own language
if your name is not an English name
the island will give you one

There's an island
that keeps thinking it's a country
keeps shouting about its honor! honor! honor!
which fills it with indignation, streaks its face with tears
to drown five thousand years of grievances
the island fashions
a TV channel its howls quake the Great Wall

There's an island
with only walls no doors
no one can leave so it's decided
it's a multinational corporation shouting about being foreign!
                        cosmopolitan! the world!
to leave you must be extra patriotic (go north! north! north!)
then shout national shame! shame! shame!
The more it yells the more envious it becomes
it rues being born in times like these   bemoans its wasted talent
resents the rich despises the poor and casts out all the good-looking
                        people
it can't poison itself fast enough with MSG and roast duck

趕快蓋一堵牆
把自己封起來
不准出不准入
除非你坐的是專機
因為島上的人
早不相信
竟然還有
這麼一（兩）個島

There's an island
hastily building a wall
to barricade itself
no exit no entry
except by private jet
because people on the island
have long since stopped believing
this island (or two)
exists

一首適合四百九十五字專欄的連載詩

我一直嚮往在床上讀書
倦了睡醒來讀書
的生活然而床單被枕的牌子就叫自由來自倫敦
遙控器射出老人雞皮的笑臉
電台節目主持人駁斥聽眾說感到無助無能就是個人的失敗
於是聽眾換了聲線棄絕徬徨套用柴玲的吶喊
據說中央電視台神聖的「他的故事」每半小時就放一次
據說老人有靈丹聽見民主自由就復活
拍拍手瞇着眼陰陰笑：「反革命暴動啊——你好！」
就在布殊打來的電話旁邊。

我自少習慣了有人約稿就寫稿沒人約稿就拉倒
一個字一毛錢沒價目不寫字的生活
我自少習慣了把心中一萬字的草稿剪輯成
四百九十五四百九十四百九十八的
小品無傷大雅供人爭辯夠不夠當上
才女的榮號電話不絕需索無聊閒扯交換這個界
那個界的流行資訊笑聲一格一格立即變成公眾
散播如鼻敏感花粉
卡片簿重疊陌生的名字再努力也記不起樣子
我對世界的認識從一部電子Filofax開始

A Serialized Poem for a Four-Hundred-and-Ninety-Five-Word Newspaper Column

I've always liked the idea of reading in bed, a life spent
falling asleep reading waking up
and reading more but my sheets and pillows are made by Liberty a
London brand
the remote control fires up a wrinkled smiling goose-flesh face
the radio host tells her listener that feeling helpless is a personal failure

so her listener changes her tune she rejects fear and takes up Chai Ling's cry
they say CCTV airs the revered "His Story" every half hour
they say there's a pill to cure old age the words democracy and freedom
revive old people
clapping their hands eyes crinkling they smile dangerously: "Hello, counter
revolutionary rioting!"
right by a telephone that's ringing it's Bush on the line.

I only ever write on assignment
my life is ten cents per word no pay no words
I've always cut my ten thousand words down to a
four-hundred-and-ninety-five ninety-four ninety-eight word
piece that's innocuous yet provocative enough to earn me
the right to call myself an Author the phone keeps ringing with rapacious
demands inane small talk
gossip exchanged about this or that field laughter line by line turning
the public
disseminated like allergenic pollen
stacks of strangers' names on business cards whose faces I can't recall
my knowledge of the world began with a digital Filofax

無城

每到一個城市
就想買套房子
每到一個地方
就想搬來長住
尋找所有想像
可想而不可能
可能而不可得
不可能的人

難民後代各處
建立窮的延伸
長住不見命長
命短更尋求家
或者家的無限
無家的無限

愈想逃避的島
成為腳下的島
天下曾經在此
正是這種曾經
或是一種以為
以為曾經天下
其實飄在天上
造成今天的無
法長住的無法
逃避或回來

No City

Whenever I visit a city
I think about buying a flat
Whenever I go to a new place
I think about settling down
I'm looking for what I imagine
the thinkable cannot be done
the doable can't be attained
impossible human

The refugees' children are far-flung
their line stretches on without end
but settling won't give you a long life
the short-lived look harder for home
the boundlessness of home
or of homelessness

The more you've an itch to escape it,
the island, the more it's your here
it's true the whole world once was here too:
in fact it is that sort of once
or maybe a sort of believing
believing this once was the world
when really it hovered in mid-air
which makes it now unthinkable
to make a home here, to leave
or to return

無法回來的城
曾經輝煌的城
無人認得的城
輝煌預言失去
歷史預言曾經
預言無人記得
期待無人認得
無人能夠留下
無樓能夠留下
無人能夠買樓
無人需要買樓
無樓能夠失去
不可能的有
不可能的樓

人這麼多
做不成人
剩下無
我們就是
無人
不是人
就是無

A city you cannot return to
a city that used to bedazzle
a city no one recognizes
they say that the dazzle portends loss
history once used to portend but
the prophecies no one remembers
a forecast that no one recalls
when no one remains
when no flats remain
when no one can buy one
when nobody buys
people not flats lose
impossible that
impossible flat

So many people
there's no way to live
what's left is no thing
that makes us
no body
if not a body
then just a no

你們與我們

現代殖民了你們
你們想做我們又
最瞧不起我們

殖民現代了我們
把文學腰骨互信歷史改
寫成理性商業靈巧法制
之方程式之唯一公義
以及自由以及華洋雜處之唯一
在我們裡面而我們
從未現代　　最瞧不起公義以及
平等　　仰賴古音古語古惑
情操託上帝觀音星座蘇
文峰遠視眼的福最不習慣
你們的從未現代

我們習慣了
面朝後面的殘骸被拖著向前衝
背對胡椒警棍有點
催淚的我們不是天使因為
我們就是
殘骸身上剝下來刮出來
一層層皮連肉加點梅菜
餵飼我們的殘障廢墟
吐出紅色的泡沫細味回甘都怪
你們今天的花
為甚麼這樣紅

You and Us

Modernity colonized you
You want to be us but
you despise us

Colonialism modernized us
It wrote literature backbone trust and history
into commerce reason the nimble formula of rule
of law of the only impartial
free place where Chinese people and foreigners lived together
inside us while we
have never been modern   of all things we looked down on justice
and equality   looked up to
classical speech classical language classic mischief
Our trust in God the Kuanyin Bodhisattva the Zodiac
fengshui master So Man Fung's gift of sight we'll never get used to
your never having been modern

We're used to
debris facing backwards while being dragged forward
our backs to the pepper police batons it's
tear-inducing we're not angels because
we are
debris   layer upon layer of skin and flesh with pickled vegetables
flayed from us picked clean
feed our crippled ruined city
spouting red bubbles if you think for a minute you'll wonder
why your flowers are
so red today

明明是大不列顛太平洋佈下的一隻
棋子　　你們明明不要我們
因為棋盤是共同利用讓
豬仔豬花買辦苦力教養出
自以為是日不落王國的哈姆雷特
要還是不要國
家　　彷彿是選擇
全世界人民的選擇
但你們與我們從來
都不是人民

我們是拿著信的
羅生克蘭和蓋登思鄧
開信就是殺頭的時
候而這封信這封信
就叫民主

Great Britain's pawn in the Pacific
it goes without saying: you abandoned us
because the chessboard is all about mutual benefit letting
the coolies flower-sellers and middlemen raise
a self-appointed Hamlet of the empire on which the sun never sets
do you or don't you want a home
land   now that's a choice
a choice open to the peoples of the world
but neither you nor we have
ever been peoples

We're the letter-bearing
Rosencrantz and Guildenstern
when the letter is opened our heads will be chopped
off and this letter this letter
is called democracy

To Octavio Paz

人相交時想像
是鷹是蛇是熊
是蜥蜴不想像
人。這是性與
色之別但太陽
文明大愛無色

人獸共性
只有人有色
有欲有欲之延
後之屈伸之置
換於是有家有
黨有國有資本

在新資本假共產之間
以詩剖開一個真共和
清空一個二百個又二
千個年輕人的國不見

家

佇立在離與留
樹的深與風的
淺之間太陽無
影無色只有詩
記得曾經有人

To Octavio Paz

When humans intertwine we imagine
we're eagles snakes bears
lizards we don't think about being
human. That's what makes sex different
from lust but the sun
is so civilized it loves without lust

Humans, like animals, are animals
but only humans lust
our desire pro
longs it expands and dis
places hence the home
party nation and capital

In the space between new capitalism and fake communism
poetry slices open a real republic
emptying out a homeland for two hundred and two
thousand young people without a

home

Poised between leaving and staying
the depth of trees and shallow
wind the sun casts no
shadow of desire only poetry
remembers once there were people here

花與路

你搞來卡夫卡這絕活我
只好勵精圖治重拾
生活的紋理。盆花沒失蹤只是
五行欠水十天了你不死我死
剪掉黃葉枯枝竟然
心裡還有翠綠的顏色

衣服被鋪都長霉了
嚴冬半途又回春
這鬼城的天氣深得
你脾氣的真傳
莫以為撒手就可不管
這城會一直抽你的水
又動氣了！你的固執
已經要了你的命
還在乎抽水與平反這
微細如游絲的分別嗎

在哀傷與虛無之間
我沒變成法國電影
（斷了氣）炸成藍色
當不成歐陸兩個女孩
不為歐陸而是我
不是女。這不是比興
是詠物而且不太現代

Potted Plants and Path

You're pulling your Kafka stunt so I have to
pull myself together and reweave
the fabric of my everyday life. The potted plants aren't lost, but
of the five elements they lack water. Ten days if you don't die I will
pruning dead leaves and branches reveals
a deeper glimmer of green

Mold on clothes and blankets
halfway through a bitter winter spring arrives
this cursed city has
inherited your temper
don't think you can wash your hands of it—
the city will bleed you dry
you've lost it again! Your stubbornness
has cost you your life
do you still care about the gossamer difference
between being bled dry and being rehabilitated

Torn between grief and nihilism
I haven't turned into an arthouse film
(Breathless) exploded into blue
not *Two English Girls and the Continent*
not because of the continent but because I'm
not a girl. This is not a metaphor it's
an ode to an object that's not exactly modern

彼岸有花。你與小津喫泡飯
與大島渚拼酒？你就好啦
你的輕，我們承受
輕輕的、輕輕的、輕輕的
那離開的瞬間，墜落的姿勢
有些符號有些記認有些
蟲鳥的品種山水的顏色
已經永遠失去了
前朝的忠臣只能失憶
又變成忠臣
你跟石堅做朋友了還是
吳楚帆？你看
林峯你說他是忠定奸？
前面的路不是路
城市迷失的人不絕
團轉但你說

緊握一隻手電筒
（LED這發明真耐用哩)只要
找對夠舊的鞋
即使再漆黑還是
可以走下去的

The far shore is in flower with *higanbana*. You're eating *zosui* with Ozu
and drinking Oshima under the table? Aren't you the lucky one
Your lightness is something we bear
lightly, lightly, lightly
In those moments of leaving, the posture of descent
some motifs some marks some
species of birds and bees and landscape colors
have already been lost forever
the previous dynasty's loyal subjects must suffer amnesia
to become loyal subjects again
Have you become friends with Shih Kien or was it
Cho-fan Ng? Does
Lam Fung look like a hero or villain to you?
The road ahead is not a road
people lost in the city
keep turning around but you said

holding an electric torch tightly
(LEDs what a useful invention) as long as
your shoes are well-worn
no matter how dark it is
you can keep on going

美好危機

我是我媽
美好生活的範例
令我對自己　以及代表我的世界
充滿狐疑　側着半邊身衝上衝下衝過一個個
長方形條狀物
扛回一籃小圓日本
天使蘋果

卜卜脆五分鐘吃完
偶而記得抬頭剪掉枯枝
旅行回來乾死一半的簕杜鵑
刮颱風整棵從天台斷枝跳樓
貓咪每天打架一隻痴肥一隻過瘦因為
一隻老要搶一隻的食物一隻又老讓一隻啃掉一盤又一盤至嘔吐不止而
貓咪從不拖地
這種生活要撐一種所謂和平安寧
門面何其難內容免問

美好更是非人能至
開一個下午的會討論副學士如何再開十五門課
金融瘦身整容下屬的大細腦
危機管理我也想唸這種學校我的
衣食父母讓我一分一秒活下去撐着我
的危機意識如此美好
我如何對我媽對你媽對世界的媽說
我確實就是
美好生活的範例
不知應是美好還是範例的覆亡

A Beautiful Crisis

I am my mother's
exemplar of a beautiful life
this fills me with suspicion of myself   and the world
that represents me   I scoot sideways around and past a series
of rectangular objects
and lug back a basket of small round Japanese
angel apples

crunch crunch in five minutes they're gone
Sometimes I remember to look up and trim the dead branches
when I got back from holiday the bougainvillea had half withered
it committed suicide by leaping off the balcony during the typhoon
the cats fight every day one is obese one is excessively thin because
one keeps stealing the other's food and the other lets it keep eating
until it throws up and
cats never mop the floor
how can anyone maintain a semblance of so-called
peace and quiet in this life never mind the content
the beautiful is humanly impossible
all afternoon I'm stuck in a meeting to discuss fifteen new courses
                        for the associate degree
financial fitness surgical enhancement employee brains
crisis management I'd like to enrol too
What keeps me alive instant by instant and keeps my
sense of crisis alive how beautiful
How can I tell my mother your mother the world's mothers that
I indeed am
the exemplar of a beautiful life
whether this is the fall of the beautiful or of the exemplary

罪貓

絕對的靜
斜斜看　月的鈎子
貓哀哀叫
為啥吾非
狗非狗非狗非狗……
立志吵醒一個自以為
地靈人傑的小島
成五千年古文明
石頭下惡貫滿盈的一記
波斯地氈

Cat Guilt

Absolute quiet
Looking sidelong   the hook of a moon
the cat wails
Why am I not a
dog not dog not dog not dog . . .
It's bent on rousing the whole
island proud of itself and its people
Five thousand years of civilization
becomes a Persian rug
oozing wickedness under every cobblestone

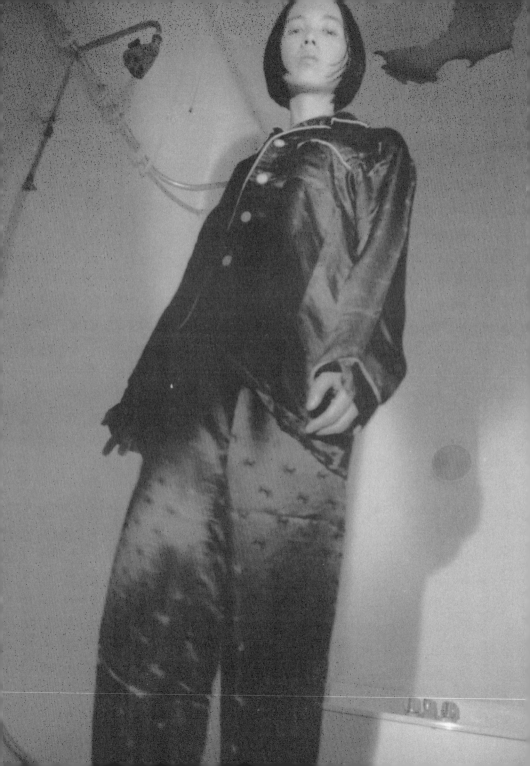

YOU 妳

轉頁

一個在等候的人跟一個在轉身的人
跟一個在戀愛中的人
本質上是一樣

我躺在床上想像妳的轉身
妳的心頁躺在鍋上斯斯響
一種墮的聲音卻被煮熟了
我指我的

我躺在床上想像
妳想像
等待我心這頁
呈金黃
香脆而不墮
如炸魚薯條

我們知道如何嗎
我們敢嗎
我們看見
敢不跟心押韻嗎

當我們忍受從那高處墜落
太高
太多心已然於葉間
於妳我腳下

一片葉輾轉
我們跌墮
於一片叫做自由的心上

Turning a Leaf

Someone waiting and someone turning round
and someone falling in love
are the same on the inside

I lie in bed imagining you turning
pages of your heart lie sizzling in a pan
a falling sound cooked through
I mean my own

I lie in bed imagining
you imagining
waiting for this page of my heart
to turn golden yellow
crisp and unfalling
like fish and chips

Don't we know how
Don't we dare
Don't we see
Doesn't brave rhyme with love

When we survive a fall from a
lofty height
too many hearts lie already the leaves
beneath your feet and mine

A leaf turns over
we fall
upon a leaf of the heart called freedom

音石

湖非承受映照
樹與雲的痛苦
湖只承受
映照的痛苦
因為她映照的
只有她自己

多少年了
我又在夢中遇到妳
這個小村落的人
彷彿都在等我來
妳在樓上奏一種不知名的樂器
是古琴嗎但忽高忽低如三絃
我佯作不認得妳
莫論琴音

走後又放不下心
只好死撐着找回去
分明是故地
卻只剩廢墟
空置的樓臺
欄杆都快要崩頹
只待我確認嗎
就可以塌下來了

多少年
仍然難以割捨
曾經痛恨的這部份自己

Notestone

A lake doesn't suffer
the heartache of reflecting trees and clouds
a lake only suffers
the heartache of reflecting
because all she reflects
is herself

Years later
I encounter you in a dream
the people in this village
are all waiting for me
you're on a balcony playing a nameless instrument
is it a *guqin*? the strings ring out abrupt highs and lows like a *sanxuan*
I pretend I don't know you
or the notes you are playing

I walk away but can't let it go
I force myself to find my way back
clearly this old haunt of mine
has turned into rubble
an empty pagoda
the railings crumbling
Are they waiting for me to register them
before collapsing

It's been years
it's hard to cast off
this part of myself I used to loathe

業已成廢墟
卻依然高低起伏
弦音漫漫
沉在湖中如石

which is already rubble
it surges and falls
each plucked note lingers
sinks into the lake like a stone

永遠

東京
我到過無數次的城市
只有迷路是永遠
在計程車司機手套永遠白
與妳的焦燥之間
回到妳家
每次都是挑戰
大家知道大家不說大家微笑大
家的距離的組織的壓力
綿密如Keio百貨公司外
長龍向我們彎腰 (非鞠躬)
絲襪永遠挺直如果她們有
選擇　她們不會向我們前傾永遠
東京　不是一種選擇
對於妳
　　　我　或者她們

Always

Tokyo
a city I've been to countless times
only getting lost is permanent
between the taxi driver's always white gloves
and your irritation
making it back to your place
is always a challenge
we know we keep quiet we smile we
both have the pressure of structure of distance of home
fastidious as the long queue of clerks outside Keio Department Store
bending (not bowing) to us
not a crease in a stocking not that these women
had a choice   or would they always be inclining in our direction
Tokyo   is not a choice
for you
    me   or them

時空

時間如影在路
英文的思念叫長
我長─長──的想妳
垂下兩隻袖兩隻褲腳伸長手指腳指伸長
每一條頭髮與眉毛
拖在地上如根
一隻黑鳥飛過
細細的影子在樹
葉子散落一地

中文的寂寞叫空
一張白白的稿紙
「喂，再來情詩三首！」
半透明沒一個影子
世界很大而我短短的
坐在這裏　愈坐愈透明
沒有文字可填滿
我四面八方的空
與前前後後的長

Spacetime

Time is like a shadow on the road
The English word longing has length in it
I long—long——for you
My sleeves pant legs lengthen fingers and toes lengthen
every single hair on my head and brow
stretches downwards trailing on the ground like banyan roots
a black bird flies by
casting its slender shadow on the tree
Leaves scatter

Loneliness in Chinese is empty
An empty sheet of lined paper
"Hey you, three more love poems!"
translucent it has no shadow
the world is big and for now I am
sitting here   growing transparent
No words can fill up
how empty I am on all sides
and, in front and behind, how long

船和反應

在茶樓中見你在煮餸　很擔心
夢　總是有很多奇怪的情緒反應
有時　只是這些反應重要
彷彿人與事之間沒了關連
彷彿我們想望的　有時候的天空
都在外面
夢中沒抬頭的空檔與反應

都在外面
飛翼船上海水兩面潑上來
皆超出身外　比人高
裡面卻是乾乾的
我抹着玻璃　水意原來
跟我一點關係都沒有
水外的城市就在前面
彷彿下着大雨
而下雨
分明已經是
昨天的事

Boat and Reaction

You were cooking in a dim sum restaurant   which was worrying
Dreams are full of strange moods and reactions
Sometimes   only these reactions matter
as if there's no connection between people and things that happen
as if the sometimes sky we imagine
is all outside
In dreams there is no space to look up and react

It's all outside
the sea is splashing up both sides of the hydrofoil
the waves beyond us   taller than us

inside it's dry
I wipe the window   the waterfulness
has nothing to do with me
The city beyond water lies straight ahead
as if it were raining hard
the rain
is already
a yesterday thing

離開

地鐵又
著火了
一地白煙
消防員螢光黃
我不斷的咳
K幸好妳不在

每一次離開
流連在妳的頸之間
上一輛的士
開去一定是錯的地方
虛脫如一部法國電影
總有女男主角
為我們重逢

Departure

The subway is
on fire again
the ground carpeted with smoke
firemen in neon yellow
I can't stop coughing
K, it's good you're not here

Every time I leave
I linger along your neck
step into a taxi
clearly headed the wrong way
exhausted like a French arthouse film
there's always a male and female lead
reuniting for us

爆谷

我把手插入
妳盈握的爆谷纍纍
溫暖如我身
點點
金黃與米白
抹拭暢泳的指頭
牛油過後
只希望它們可再長一點
我指我的手指

把點滴放進口中
珍惜咬下去的力度
彷彿跟妳
說——不，呼喊——
親愛的，這只是
爆谷呢

Popcorn

I reach my hand
into the overflowing
popcorn you hold
warm like my body,
flecks of
gold and white
on my buttered fingertips,
wishing they were longer—
I mean my fingers.

I place a piece into my mouth,
savoring the force of each bite,
as if to say
—no, calling out—
Dear, it's only
popcorn.

月

因為妳不懂方塊字
我無法跟妳說這些
有一種時間
十五的月亮永遠是滿的
初一是彎
而且從新開始　但
是的　我來自的地方
亦不講這些

妳托著下巴　髮在擺：
為什麼我們的時間
總是忘記了月光？
讓我下種時
無法給洋蔥、青椒及紫蘇
圓它們生命的圈——
這刻鐘妳的髮散落如Pollock的秋
滑入
不是妳又不是我的時間內
有人忙著談星的膨脹即收縮
在黑洞內妳我高速迴旋如意大利麵
二月為什麼受歧視
妳卻在與綿被運轉
逞強的唇：不要以為我沒有
努力著撐起眼皮

Mona
忘了告訴妳
我們的month
亦是moon的意思

Moon

Because you can't read Chinese characters
there's no way I can tell you that
in this way of telling time
the moon is always full on the fifteenth
The first of the month is a crescent
a new start   but
yes   where I'm from
we don't talk about this either

Your head cupped in your hands   you toss your hair:
why does our way of telling time
always forget the moonlight?
I've no way to complete the circles of life
when planting
onions and peppers and perillas
In this moment your hair is splattered like a Pollock autumn
sliding
into a time that's neither yours nor mine
someone is busy talking about stars expanding, which is to say contracting
while we spin like spaghetti in a black hole
what have you got against February
you and the quilt spinning
stubborn lips: don't think I'm not
straining to keep my eyelids open

Mona,
I almost forgot to say
our *month*
also means *moon*

相看

船上有妳
看着船下眾生如我
隨時反肚
而妳把一尾一尾
反過來反過去救活
讓水的壓力　輕輕推開
化成可褪下的鱗羽

學習改變心的形狀
好抵禦頑強的濁流
回到本來柔軟的身體
為被溺斃的細胞
作人工呼吸
不需要力氣
如魚回到
水中活過來　看着妳
在水上微笑

Eyes Meet

You're on a boat
watching as the creatures below like me
go belly up
You flip them back over
one by one
gently breaking   the surface tension
turning into fading scales

I'll learn to change the shape of my heart
to brave the turgid current
Returning to what was a soft body
Performing CPR on
drowning cells
doesn't require strength
just as fish are revived
once returned to water   watching as
above the water you smile

抱

抱着妳
用最貼近的狐度
學習貓的柔軟
在牠殘暴完我們家附近
所有蝴蝶之後
心安理得地
回歸妳的圓
內裡有一顆非常非常小
安靜但
跳動非常非常大的
圓心
如果剛好環抱
一起跌進黑洞時
便不會丟掉
即使失重

Embrace

I embrace you
at an angle that mimics
the arc of a cat's softness
After savaging
the neighborhood butterflies
it's content to return to
your roundness
Inside it a teeny-tiny
quiet little
so hard-beating
core
If we embrace
while falling into a black hole
we'll never lose each other
even weightless

遠

需要疏遠
一點點
為好好
想念
退到牆與
牆之間的
地氈末端
冰將溶又重新
凝住　與念黏起來

還原我
剛好
看到完整
如妳

Distance

Keep
a little distance
to make
the heart grow fonder
Withdraw to the
edge of the
walled in carpet
the ice will melt and
refreeze   into frisson

Restore me
there I saw
completeness
like you

我裏面

是跟妳一起
我發現自己的大
妳說：妳有一部份
自足自成　　妳之為妳
非我可觸　　也不便打擾
我轉轉眉：明明可把一切給妳
不可以想像哪條頭髮下面
有空位　　但我錯了
總有某一個彎位某一處手指頭舔過的某一點
想妳來但容不下
有了妳便不成為我
之為我之為妳
而妳從外探頭進來
又縮回去
貓頭貓腦的看我
等門再打開換一幅風景
讓妳走進來
剛剛好

Inside Me

is together with you
I discover my vastness
You say: there's part of you
that's self-contained   your being you
not something I can touch   or disturb
I arch my eyebrows: of course I could give you everything
not a hair on my head
would have space beneath it   But I'm mistaken
there's always a curve a fingertip you licked a cranny
that longs for you but can't contain you
With you, I'm no longer me
being me being you
You peek your head in
and shrink back
observing me catheadedly
waiting for the door to open a new landscape
precisely in time for
you to walk in

PROSE POEMS 散文詩

家私奏鳴曲

「事情已經變得很複雜。」燈光總是不夠明亮。叫人無法辨認透明的事物。在暗閣中尋找鮮明的紋理。風沙刮起就蓋上紅布展示厚道。天朗氣清你看看頭頂那倒下來的聲音。遙遠有孩子的啼哭混在電視廣播中。雪白的牆壁由光明步向沉默。暴風雨後窗上污垢的痕跡逐漸顯現。(有鋼鐵碰着鋼鐵的聲音，等待迴響。)桌上的攝影機哪裏去，一直以為是亂了後來發現被偷去。於是關起窗來門上裝置鎖鏈。窗簾拉起不惜減低透明度。不如安裝射燈補補光線照亮你想照亮的事物。照亮回音(萬一來了)成輕淺的剪影。照亮出破碎

坐在這裏書寫顫抖。在反覆的冷氣機與消息之間呼吸。電話無法舒展失去攝影機的空白。電視厭倦長途電話的定格，反抗起來播了鄰台的衛星。傳真機的資訊突破了垃圾桶的防線。廣場上露營觀望太陽升降。垃圾桶中唯獨缺乏垃圾

一幅一幅的影像更替。一模一樣的顏色在升降臂上上落。甚麼都沒發生過哩。遊客的攝影機在廣場閃動。最後一個悲劇英雄接過黑幕下的框架，奉命清洗刷不去的墨跡。

Private Furniture Sonata

"It's all become so complicated." The light in your home is never bright enough. You can't make out anything transparent. You search for distinct patterns in the darkness. A gust of sand and wind, spread out the red cloth as a thick kindness. On clear days you watch the crash of something falling from above. The distant sound of a child crying mingles with a television broadcast. White walls step from brightness into silence. Streaks of dirt emerge on windows after the storm. (There's a metallic clang of iron against iron, awaiting its echo.) The camera on the table disappeared. You thought it was misplaced but it turned out to have been stolen. So you shut the windows and put a chain on the door. You draw the blinds even though it makes the world less transparent. How about putting in a spotlight to illuminate whatever you want to illuminate. To illuminate the echo (if it comes) and give it a pale silhouette. Illuminate the broken

Sit here writing and shivering. Breathing between the repetitions of the air conditioner and the news. The phone can't reach far enough to fill up the blankness of where the camera was. The television is tired of how long-distance calls freeze, so it's acted up and started playing the next satellite channel. The fax machine breaks through the garbage can's defences. Camp out on the Square to watch the sun rise and set. The only thing the rubbish bin is missing is rubbish

One image replenishes another. The exact same color goes up and down the crank. Like nothing happened. The tourists' cameras flash on the Square. The last tragic hero reaches out to take the frame draped in heavy black cloth, under orders to scrub indelible ink stains clean.

包浩斯庸俗化實習

情形是這樣的。最近搬了屋。已經是半年前的事了。在這屋裡總是情緒低落，因為有一些基本問題。燈光太暗。要加一盞檯燈在書桌：一盞床頭燈——但是沒床頭櫃——一盞座地燈：靠窗的地方也應該有一盞。太多了，安三個射燈頭在三個位置中間，一左一右一向下。怎樣取一個平衡？要度一度。一排射燈頭在頭頂，黑色，在白牆上，路軌？考慮黑與白之間的一系列顏色。太曖昧。坦白講，這些燈頭的形狀總是不夠圓。要裝一個遙控器調校它的圓度。有石英跳字顯示光線角度那種。

抬頭想象燈，想到了，微笑，大笑，肚子餓了，站起來，去找食物。這屋子地板的紙皮石圖案呈長方形，為二十厘米x十厘米，非常憫悶的棕色。每走一步，從一隻腳腳跟至另一隻腳腳趾公的尖端共有六塊長方形的闊度。八塊太危險，五塊太反動。如果每一步都如此，理想世界是很近。

近了，雞翼，太想吃雞翼。吃雞翼也有很多種吃法。一隻雞翼也有各不相同的部份。用酒浸，用火烤，用新歷聲高科技輸送入來的噪音。微波電子中溫鍋。雞翼，死未？我拿著叉篤著腋下。噗噗噗血水混在奶白醺香的雙蒸裡，淡出，好味道。

Bauhaus Exercise in Vulgarization

So this happened. You moved house. Half a year ago. Fundamental problems with the place are making you depressed. The lights are too dim. You need a desk lamp for the desk, a bedside lamp—even though you don't have a bedside table—and a floor lamp, plus one by the window. That's too many, so you might get three spotlights and mount them centrally, pointing left right and downwards. How to balance them out? Measure the space. A row of spotlights overhead, black on a white wall, like train tracks? Consider the colors between black and white. Too ambiguous. None of these bulbs are ever round enough. Get a remote control for their roundness. The kind with a quartz display for the lighting angle.

Now you look up, picture possible lights, settle on some, smile, laugh out loud, you're hungry, stand up and look for food. The mosaic flooring is rectangular 20 cm x 10 cm tiles in the drabbest brown. One step, from the heel of one foot to the tip of the other foot's big toe, measures six tile widths. Eight would be too dangerous and five too reactionary. If every step could be like this, the ideal world would be close at hand.

It's near, chicken wings, you're craving chicken wings. Which there are many ways of eating. A single wing is composed of many different parts. Marinate in wine, grill, pipe in high tech stereo amplified noise. Braise in the microwave. Chicken wings again?! Poke a fork into its armpit. Blood streams into the milky whiteness of double distilled baijiu. It diffuses, yum.

(1989)

包浩斯庸俗化實習

情形是。最近搬屋。已經是半年前的事。
屋裏總是情緒低落，因為有一些基本問題
燈光太暗。要加一盞檯燈在書桌一盞床頭
燈但是沒床頭櫃一盞座地燈—靠窗的地方
也應該有一盞。太多了，安裝三個射燈在
三個位置中間，一左一右一向下。怎樣取
平衡?量一量。一排射燈頭在頭頂，黑色
白牆上，路軌?考慮黑與白之間一系列顏
色。太曖昧。坦白講這些燈罩的形狀總不
夠圓。裝一個遙控器調校圓度。石英跳字
顯示光線角度那種。亮，很亮。太亮給人
壓力
會爆

抬頭想像燈想到，微笑，大笑，肚子餓了
站起來找食物。地板紙皮石圖案呈長方形
為二十厘米 x 十厘米，憫悶的棕色走一步
從一隻腳腳跟至另一隻腳大拇趾的尖端共
有六塊長方形的寬度。八塊太危險，五塊
太反動。如果每一步都如此，理想世界很
近

近了，雞翼，太想吃雞翼。雞翼有很多種
吃法。同一隻雞翼不相同的各部。酒泡火
烤，新歷聲高科技輸送微波電子震盪。雞
翼，死了沒？叉子插其腋下噗噗噗血水混
在奶白醺香的雙蒸酒裏淡出
好味道

Bauhaus Exercise in Vulgarization

It's like this. You moved house. Half a year ago.
In this house, fundamental problems are making you depressed
The lights are too dim. You need a desk lamp on the desk a bedside
lamp even sans bedside table and a floor lamp—plus one by
the window. That's too many, so you might get three spotlights
and mount them centrally, pointing left right and downwards. How
to balance them out? Measure. A row of spotlights overhead, black
on a white wall, like train tracks? Consider the colours between black
and white. Too ambiguous. None of these bulbs are ever round
enough. Get a remote control for their roundness. The kind with a
quartz display for the lighting angle. It's bright. Very bright. So bright
the pressure
might explode you

Now you look up, picture possible lights, settle on some, smile,
laugh out loud, you're hungry stand up and look for food. The
mosaic flooring is rectangular 20 cm x 10 cm tiles, drab brown steps
from the heel of one foot to the tip of the other foot's big toe six
tile widths. Eight would be too dangerous, five too reactionary. If
every step could be like this, the ideal world would be close
at hand

It's near, chicken wings, you're craving chicken wings. Which there
are many ways of eating. The same wing has many different parts.
Marinated in wine grilled High tech stereoed microwave vibrated.
Chicken wings again?! Poke a fork into its armpit. Blood streams
into the milky whiteness of double distilled baijiu
yum

(2020–2021)

上海麵的生長

待燈光陸續消散就走回船艙去，或是冷了。坐下來尋找一個位置然後
發現這裡光線不足寫起字來手影遮住半張紙。眼睛有點睜不開來。或
者需要找點甚麼做就記起一個朋友，問我每天乘船的方便與不便。很
久沒見他吧看見的時候也在黑暗中。我翻著包包中的雞皮袋一個個揭
開一張張剪紙撕出一角memo不知是誰的電話丟掉。昏黃的文字有老去
的資訊我擔心的教育改革各種傾側的反應箝在中間。會不會也箝住你
我(噢卻特赦了全人類)的生長。一張張剪報一段段疊住一個中大的朋
友拍的一張罷課的照片。真是湊巧。怎麼說呢。這片地方，與它的，
艱難的生長。(我丟掉的號碼會不會有人拾起來打過去就找到要找的
人？)

其實船很快就到岸，有時候太快。總欠缺寫一篇論香港教育改革的文
字瞄一陣又寫一首詩的足夠剩餘。(對面的女孩帶著一隻耳環是一條彈
簧。)懷念碼頭旁一片上海小店的三絲冷麵，我媽媽弄得好好的冷麵後
來便不弄了我抱怨她又抱怨是為了沒市場。沒市場？我走進去坐下嗯
今次的醋下多了──但冷麵的未來還是好的，我瞪著這隻圓得無懈可
擊的碟子想想還是不相信打包，想起的人吃不下了。(我憑什麼相信冷
麵的未來包括它的廚師與觀眾如我的味覺？)

Shanghai Noodles Grow Up

Back to the cabin when the lights dim and flicker out. Maybe I'm cold. I sit down and look about for a spot but it's too dark, my writing hand leaves half the page in shadow. Eyelids grow heavy. I should be doing something, but then I think of a friend who asked me if taking the ferry every day is convenient. I haven't seen him in ages and when I last did it was dark. I leaf through the manila envelopes in my backpack, flipping through the cuttings they contain, tearing off the corner of a memo who knows whose phone number I've lost. The yellowing words carry stale news of disquieting educational reforms, with topsy-turvy reactions clipped inside. Is it also clipping off your and my growing up (while offering amnesty to the rest of humanity). One by one, the newspaper cuttings pile up, a friend's photo of a classroom walkout at the Chinese University. What a coincidence. How can I put it. This place and the difficulty of its growing up. (Will someone find the number I lost and get through to just the person they were looking for?)

The ferry reaches the shore soon enough, sometimes too soon. Can't ever write a piece about educational reform, nap a little, and write a poem with time to spare. (The girl sitting opposite me is wearing one earring, a spring coil.) I'm hankering after the cold noodles in the Shanghai noodle shops by the ferry, my mother used to make wonderful cold noodles but then she stopped making them, I grumbled at her and she grumbled about the lack of demand. Lack of demand? I go inside sit down and oops too much vinegar this time. But cold noodles still have a future. I stare at the flawlessly round plate. I don't believe in takeaway because the person I have in mind will already be full. (Why do I believe in the future of Shanghai cold noodles, their chef, and the taste buds of an audience like me?)

致友人

電話響的時候知道是你，拿起的時候就趕快說喂是你你你好嗎。然後又太趕你又在趕於是你我都笑了。我問喂你怎樣啦你答你怎樣啦才真，彷彿問問怎樣啦對方便好了。我們多少年沒有見了。(我在看一齣叫一個男人和一個女人的法國電影。) 男人怎樣啦。在睡，每天回來都看他睡。噢他叫乜乜東。不可以說，一說他便醒。他的性情跟我相像興趣跟你相類，所以沉悶得不得了。晚上常有一千隻飛機在天花板。想不到我們跑了十萬八千哩談這些。在相同的國卻這麼遠。那個誰綁個話筒在眼鏡以頭當鼓我也想。午夜醒來告訴自己這便是藝術了它底渺茫的意義與限制。別怨如果你相信你所做的你根本沒有選擇對不對。如果不相信你我怎會遇上。(我們有機會見面嗎。) 我不知道也許在你我知道自己在幹啥的時候可以互相交換地方了。好嗎。你好嗎。保重。九月十四

To a Friend

When the phone rang I knew it would be you, so I picked up and hurriedly said hello it's you you how are you? I was in a rush and so were you so then we both ended up laughing. I said how are you doing and you said how are you doing, as if that's all we had to say. It's been years. (Well right now I'm watching a French film, *Un homme et une femme*.) How's your man? He's sleeping, this is what I do every day when I get home, watch him sleep. What's his name again? Can't say it out loud it'll wake him up. He's like me personality wise but he has more in common with you, that's why he's so boring. At night there are 1000 Airplanes on the Roof. I can't believe we're talking about this thousands of miles apart. In the same country but so far away. That so-and-so strapped a mike to her glasses and used her head as a drum, I should be doing that too. When I wake up in the middle of the night I tell myself this is art, this is art's nebulous meaning and limitations. Don't say that, you believe in what you do, you don't have a choice. If you didn't believe in it how could we ever have met. (Are we going to see each other?) I don't know maybe when both of us know what we're doing we can swap locations. Yes let's. How are you doing. Take care. September 14th

DEATH AND ADVENTURE 亡命與半途

我是一隻腳

要交一行字的生平
迫我瞪起老花眼看著
游靜是甚麼
我總是過度扮演自己
一些物事　作業　喜與不喜的
有限重覆
不及風花　貓甚至草
無我故無限
沒一隻腳踩進同一條河
踩進與拔出之間　腳已變
如何成為這隻腳
承受每次踩進與拔出　每一分
不一樣的河
腳的每一分
也化解成河

I am a Foot

I have to turn in a one-line biography
which forces my presbyopic middle-aged eyes to take a hard look at
what Yau Ching is
I am always over-acting the part
some things   some tasks   some likes and dislikes
on limited repeat
unlike wind flowers   cats or even grass
There is no me therefore I have no limits
a foot cannot step twice into the same river
before it steps out   it has already become a different foot
how to become this foot
how to bear each stepping in and out   every moment
the river is different
every inch of the foot
has already become the river

預習

未知生焉知
　　不能復生視　　如歸　　而無憾
出生入　一線間　生契濶
輕於鴻毛　　而後已而復生
不瞑目不足惜
寧　　不屈鳴不默
一雞一鳴撐飯蓋鴨升天
憂患不終無安樂　　啦　　啦啦
未　　得呢你就想

Trial Run

        as a door-nail
        and gone   to the world
        air   broke drop
nothing is certain but   and taxes
        mask   knell   grip
        blow   metal   rattle
food for worms sticky end brown bread
        or alive valiant to the   la   la la
wish I were   yeah right you wish

公路

如果一直走總會有意外
路長且直突然有彎角
持穩駕駛盤需要定定的勇氣
思念長且直需要定定的勇氣
如果一直去總會有意外
我累了
在公路旁被遺棄的衣服
輾過一頭飛鳥的殘骸無法辨認
翼與心的距離
當你在公路上你無法停下來
公路駕著車車駕著人
生不過是思念的延伸
如果一直去總會有意外
忽然停下來總會有意外

Highway

Keep driving and you'll crash
a long straight road suddenly veers
a steady hand on the wheel takes an unblinking courage
a long straight longing takes an unblinking courage
keep going and you'll crash
now I'm flagging
clothes abandoned by the highway
a bird carcass crushed unrecognizable
distance from the wing to the heart
When you can't pull over on the highway
driving cars driving people on the highway
life is just an extension of longing
keep going and you'll crash
stop abruptly and you'll crash

我們如此結識

但願我可以沒成長
完全憑直覺覓對象
「橋可能是冰了」

「橋」是往高速公路的入口
或出口
美文一望無際
總是似乎甚麼都可能
然「可能」實指「大概」呢
到你睇定定無走雞啦時
一定經已冰封三尺

也非一日之寒
看見便是太遲
錯得超乎我想像
以時速八十五哩九十哩滑行
只要煞掣　如此敏捷　乾淨
一刀兩斷的方式

一隻手　兩隻手都放開
呔盤自己會
高速旋轉的
敏捷乾淨一望無涯的方式
你卻說如此力氣不如施於人
通街BB肥的男孩
短波褲蕩漾　從棒球賽出來
坦露堅實不生癌的乳
在街上相互推笑著
咱們趁開著車況且難得夠打今次

That's How We Met

If only I didn't have to grow up
if only I had an instinct for falling in love
"the ramp might be icy"

Onramp to or
offramp from the highway
boundless American English
always makes anything seem possible
the possible is really a maybe
and by the time you can see it there's no escape
yes it's iced over

this is more than a day's worth
if you can see it it's too late
an unfathomable mistake
if you're spinning out at eighty or ninety miles an hour
all you have to do is brake suddenly   it'll be swift   clean
and ruthless

One hand   both hands let go
the steering wheel
starts spinning of its own accord
cleanly boundlessly
you said if you're so strong then take it out on someone
the teenage boys with baby fat roaming the streets
in their rippling shorts   streaming out of baseball games
baring firm uncancerous breasts
shoving each other and laughing on the streets
since we're driving and we're more than a match for them let's

敏捷乾淨又一股作氣的方式
超乎我想像
忘卻又記得的事情
我們如此結識嗎

I-94東
往湖的路
今天封了
見冰不見湖一望無邊的日子皚皚
走得太快到盡頭時……
抑或永沒盡頭？
改道改道改道箭嘴指向東又指向西
我又到了I-94西跟東一模一樣
車的王國USA
還是自動的王國？
模糊地迷戀妳一場
就當風雨下潮漲
我的車自動震
是太冷太快太滑太亂太感動還是根本不想幹
哥哥究竟你在唱啥

一望無涯的是雪是愛是公路還是USA
冰封的橋
與我無關的速度
在快門與煞掣之間用力
車子高速旋轉如棒球　回家了
這樣乾淨爽快一望……
曾忘掉這種遐想
就當風雨下潮漲

我們如此結識

swiftly cleanly and immediately
it's unfathomable
the things we've forgotten and now remember
Is that how we met

The I-94 East
towards the lake
is closed today
you can see the ice but not the lake   boundless days glinting
if you go too fast and reach the end . . .
or is there ever an end?
detours detours detours the arrow points east and west
I'm back on the I-94 West is just the same as East
the kingdom of cars, America,
or the kingdom of automation?
I fell hazily in love with you
let's call it the tide rising in a storm
the car's shaking automatically
is it too cold too fast too slippery too messy too romantic or just fuck it
bro whatcha singing

What's boundless, snow love highways or the USA
the icy ramp
the impersonal speed
exert force between the accelerator and the brake
the car will spin like a baseball   you'll be home
it'll be clean swift and bound . . .
I'd forgotten this fantasy
let's call it the tide rising in a storm

That's how we met

認影

我又回到老地方
椅子愈來愈舒適了
頃刻暗掉的冷空氣
與音效八方包裹你
跟盯住你的目光一起
化成牆紙
只有不停的影子是真實
這就叫安全
現實一切都不重要了
觀眾不會生老病死
你在的地方不需要電影了嗎
沒戲院何以安身豈言立命?
沒跟過漆黑的陌生人
搓捏談情如何長成
有影子的人
但你不再需要影了

暫借的安慰為何不散
在你我贖回影子的一點
驟暗忽明中曾經彼此相認

Shadow of Recognition

I'm back in old haunts
The chairs are more and more comfortable
the chilled air dims instantly
it wraps you acoustically from eight sides
with the gaze fixed on you
it turns into wallpaper
only shadows that don't stop are real
this is what you'd call security
reality doesn't matter now
the audience won't age or die
do they not need movies where you are
without cinemas how can you survive, let alone live?
without having fumbled or flirted with
strangers in the dark how can anyone
grow up to cast a shadow
well you don't need one now

Why doesn't the borrowed comfort fade
in the flicker of us both redeeming
our shadows we used to recognize each other

看不見的人

——給小克

現在我跟所有人
一樣手閒下來就是刷
手機無意
義的無盡
背包不再帶書
與攝影機與原
稿紙有時連筆都
無眼睛十八小時的無
意義或生
命

現在我的眼與攝影機永遠
看不見你與你的崩牙你的
Lomo你的煙味你一身永遠
的黑背牆屈膝證明膝蓋的
無痛整個人陷入牆中陷入
無但唯一的屈膝現在都
看不見了

我們三十年的交錯你
替我出版的第一本書
每次看著我一直吃一直
微笑如山每年我收到的
黑白攝影年卡不絕提醒
資本財產家庭職場屈膝的
不必陷入社交顏色的社會

Invisible Man

For K. H.

Like everyone else
whenever I have a hand to spare, I swipe
phones are aim
less infinite
no more books in my backpack
no camera or fool
scap or even an eyeless
pen eighteen hours of aimless
or lifeless
ness

Now my eyes and camera will never
see you your broken tooth or
Lomo your cigarette smoke you're always
wearing black your back-to-the-wall knees bent prove
they don't hurt sink into the wall into
nothingness your only knee
has vanished

We've crisscrossed thirty years you
put out my first book
when you look at me you're always eating always
smiling like a mountain every new year
your monochrome greeting card reminds me
that buckling under capitalism property family and career
is not required caving to the colors of socializing social

認可的不必
絕種的人

你低頭向我唯一的
出櫃永遠的少年玩伴用你
永遠的黑與克懷抱與撞擊
社會各種暗櫃的各種交錯
與不必
你的黑
生的難與
克難都
歸於塵煙的
無盡

因為你
我願意相信
靈魂即使看不見
相信我們會
再見即使在
生命本來的無
意義中

recognition is not required
an extinct species

Your head bowed my only uncloseted
always childhood playmate in your
forever black, you hug and collide
with all society's closets and all its crisscrossing
and non-requirements
with your black
the darkness
the hardness of being alive
returns to
smoke and
nothingness

Because of you
I am willing to believe
in the soul even if invisible
yes we'll meet
again in
life's first mean
inglessness

十月

一九八八年　　不要以為
十月　　過了還會回來
除非有十一月

九月

駱駝上的搖鈴
剛剛鎖住你的銀鍊
一隻耳環的心情
拍打床褥的聲音
有床單的眼睛闔上　　別轉整塊臉
你退到月光照不到的角落
不要看見愚蠢的九月

八月

為了各樣平白並不愚蠢的理由
需要控制
一如其他月份

October

1988   don't assume
October   having gone will ever return
except in November

September

the camel's bell
clasped your silver necklace
one earring's mood
someone's beating a mattress
eyes with coverlets closing   don't turn your whole face
retreat to a corner the moon can't reach
don't look at foolish September

August

For all kinds of mundane and not at all foolish reasons
it has to be curbed
like the other months

對一塊牛扒的道德性推理

如果
要我揀
吃你　或者
愛你
我想　還是
愛你　比較　划算
因為　不吃你比吃你省力
愛你
卻
剛
相
反

Ethical Reasoning Directed at a Steak

If
I had to choose between
eating you   and
loving you
I think
loving you   would be   the better bargain
because   not eating you takes less work
than eating you
but love
works
the
other
way
round

不可能的愛

我是最被高估又
最被低估
其實我不知我是甚麼

自從有你就有我但
有你不一定有我因為
你最怕就是我

全靠我　無數字、光、色生成但
你看見這些看不見我

更要命的　是你以我之名出產那堆沒完沒了
吵到我暈的婚禮節慶壽宴告解領洗喪葬大龍鳳
好幫你逃避我以我
之名嚇死我阿彌陀

卻是在最濕冷的角落踟躕幽秘處
我伺機匍匐
當你忘了我名字忘了身
分性別年齡銀行戶口號碼手-手-腳-腳
穿過黯黑的鏡子瞥見毛孔毛髮也許
你鼻子會觸到我祝君早安

而你一定知道一定拒絕
在九千九百種自由的化身中你要
的你不會得到
你明明可得的你一定堅持錯認

Impossible Love

I am the most overrated and
underrated
I don't know what I am

Ever since there was you there's been me but
you don't entail me because
you're terrified of me

all because of me   countless words, lights, hues came into being
you see them but you can't see me

What's worse   you use my name to produce a ceaseless
pile of deafening wedding holiday birthday baptism funeral
announcements
so you can elude and
frighten me, *amitābha*

In the dankest corner the most forgotten quietest place
I'm curled up and waiting
for you to forget my name, forget id
entity sex age bank account number hands and feet
you'll glimpse my pores and hair through the dark mirror maybe
the tip of your nose will touch me good morning sir

You must know you must decline
in your nine thousand nine hundred free incarnations you won't
get what you want
and what you can get you'll insist on mistaking

如你僥倖勇
敢與我與
自己相認
也必定是太遲

If you're lucky and plu
cky enough to recognize me
and yourself
it will still be too late

你在

時與你一起我
總不在你盯著
連續劇我捧著
書刷著手機想著你的
氣味「媽咪你
上次洗頭是
幾」兩個禮拜前
才洗過冬天洗這
麼密容易……我
用了一生逃
離這種
味到你漸漸不
在時我
伸手拉住抱
住抓住這一切
你我的曾經
變得史前無例的
在

一片葉子一
碰便

When You're

here and we're together I'm
not really there you're watching
soap operas I'm reading
a book scrolling on my phone thinking of your
smell "Mum your hair
when was the last time
you" two weeks ago
can't wash it
more than that in winter . . . I've
spent my whole life running
away from this
smell but now that you're slipping
away I
stretch out my hand to
grasp it, embrace it
catch hold of it all
your and my past
has become an unprecedented
present

a leaf that once you
touch it

年少的詩

　　　　———世紀末的生長

我在Haight-Ashbury看一齣討論希皮的電影
大贈送一套列根夫婦勸人服毒的短片，他們說美國未來的希望都剩下兩
　　　　　　　　　　　　　　　　　　　　　　元，遲疑著
用來買杯Espresso是否太危險
一面讀米和斯的《三藩市灣區所見》，說：「我在這裡。」
我在這裡，而且知道得這樣少，
少到在成為物質以前也跟物質一樣甚麼都不知道。
你立即反駁，「藝術不斷向我們認知的局限挑戰」
人跟物質之間是未知與不知的距離，這是無限。
我想說，我
不知道。
或者。

你知道嗎。我想問希皮文化會否是美國中產階級
發明的一種逸樂主義的變奏呢。也有
懦弱。盲目。宣洩無法安撫的良知。替世紀的憤怒
注射嗎啡針。「Life is groovy; life is cool,
I make myself a swimming pool.」
這單純如顏色的禮儀。我遲疑，你
不知道，你的
成就。這爿土地，一直是游泳池
涼快

Poem About Being Young

—Growing up at the end of the century

At a movie about hippies in Haight-Ashbury
they played a short by the Reagans on doing drugs.
Two bucks is all that's left of America's hope for the future they said.
                              Can I risk
spending it on an espresso.
All the while I'm reading *Visions from San Francisco Bay* by Milosz. "I am here,"
I am here. There's so little I know,
so little that before I become matter I'll be as ignorant as matter.
"Art is always challenging the limits of our knowing," you respond,
the difference between man and matter is the difference between the as yet
                              unknown and the unknowable. Infinity.
I don't know, I
want to say.
Maybe.

Do you know? I want to ask: is hippie culture a variation on hedonism
invented by the American middle class. Cowardice.
Obliviousness. Let an implacable conscience vent. Injecting
morphine into a century of rage. "Life is groovy,
life is cool, I make myself a swimming pool."
A courtesy pure as color. I hesitate, oh
you don't know what you've
accomplished. This piece of land has always been swimming pool
cool

也有人
在池旁走，遲疑，想
「今天，無疑是難了。」難得過
嗎啡針嗎。但你知道生命在末世以後會繼續
生長。你知道嗎。

海鳥睜大眼搶食。我看不見亞極策斯，從前的監獄
島，今天的遊客區。你問：「香港在一九九八會
怎麼樣呢？」
(布殊也忘記所有顏色侵略的的日期，他會說：
「這又是跟我當總統毫無關係的事情。」)
「我們正在爭取一套比較⋯⋯獨立的制度。」
你著迷，立即
明白。我不是沒有
後悔的。你們總是聽見
獨立，聽不見
比較，莫論⋯⋯

三藩市的霧忘記時間。以及它帶來的一切。
(這樣真的好一點嗎？) 在我們也成為霧，或者
物質以前。繼續生長。
以及它帶來的一切。
為甚麼怕痛呢。遲早我們
都有不痛的機會
遲早當顏色
文字、布與霧
都過去，我希望，我們還可以回
頭說，我們真的
不知道

一如我們知道
甚麼

Someone else is
walking by the pool, hesitating, thinking,
"Today will be trying." More so than
morphine? You know after the apocalypse life will keep
growing? Do you know.

Wide-eyed seagulls fight over scraps. I can't see Alcatraz, the former prison
island, present-day tourist trap. "What's going to happen to Hong Kong
in 1998?" you ask.
(Bush forgot when all the colors invaded too,
"this has nothing to do with my presidency," he'd say.)
"We're fighting for a more . . . independent system."
You're sold, you get it
right away. It's not like I have
no regrets. You guys always hear
the word *independent*, and never hear
the *more*, never mind the . . .

The fog in San Francisco forgets time. Forgets everything it brings.
(Does that help?) Before we turn into fog or
into matter. Keep growing.
Forget everything it brings.
Why fear pain. Sooner or later
we'll all get to cease feeling pain
When colors, bushes and fog
fade, I hope we'll look
back and say, we really
didn't know

what do we ever
really know

未知

病原是　出生入死
一線間　做一隻
活雞撐着吃飯
要換來另一隻雞鳴
餘下沒契濶的人
才會怕比泰山重
走比留易
無憾是不可能　如歸更難
不瞑目好難看
一把灰不足惜一撒手
不外乎碰上一鼻子鴨黃色

歹活不需勇氣
修練終極好死
學習不怕死
才有知生的可能

Unknown

Illness is walking a line between
life and death   you're
a live chicken pecking at feed
to live until another cock crows
that leaves the people who've never said goodbye
only they fear shuffling off
it's easier to slip away than to stay
dying without regrets is impossible   dying well is even harder
you'll want your eyes closed
you'll want just a handful of ashes
to rub your nose in their yellowness

Living badly does not require courage
preparing for a good death
learning not to fear death
is the only way to know life

散則成風

說了太多人類的壞話
結果被人類殺掉
也很公平

（旅人問和尚：你想必不寂寞？
和尚答：你說的寂寞意思是
疲倦？你也許還不疲倦？）

沒有比死更寂寞
我從不怕寂寞
為何會怕死
不過是一件需要
一個人完成的
眾多事情之一
之最後

（可能，只是不懂得疲倦
明明路過，卻戀上路旁的石頭
忘了石也言倦，散則成風）

只是
這事完了
沒有 debrief
沒有 follow-up
沒法於世交代

Dissolve into Wind

If you constantly gripe about humanity
and humans decide to off you
that's only fair

(Traveler to monk: don't you ever get lonely?
Monk: by lonely do you mean
tired? And you, aren't you tired?)

There's nothing lonelier than death
I've never been afraid of loneliness
so why would I fear death
it's only a thing that
has to be
After all the other things you do on your own,
the very last

(Maybe you don't know how to be weary
Passing by you fell in love with stones by the wayside
you'd forgotten that stones speak of tiredness, dissolve into wind)

It's just that
it's over
no debrief
no follow-up
no explaining yourself

完成的過程
一件無法改良累積
承傳檢討回看
一下子的事

難怪歷史

there's something that
while being completed
can't be improved accumulated
inherited revisited

it's no wonder history is so

Notes

That's How We Met
The lines "If only I didn't have to grow up/if only I had an instinct for falling in love"(and two of those later in the poem, "I fell hazily . . . storm") quote Leslie Cheung's 1996 song "A Man of Intention," with lyrics by Albert Leung.

Shadow of Recognition
With thanks to the Poetry Translation Centre, where Chenxin Jiang led a workshop that produced a collective translation of this poem. The workshop's translation, "Electric Shadows," is available at www.poetrytranslation.org; this translation is Jiang's.

Invisible Man
Cheung King Hung (1949–2016), aka K.H., Hong Kong poet and photographer.

Image Credits

Frontis: Still from *Ho Yuk* (Yau Ching, 35mm film, 2002)
viii: Detail from *Ho Yuk* poster (Yau Ching, 35mm film, 2002)
xxii–1: Still from *Ho Yuk* (Yau Ching, 35mm film, 2002)
32: Still from *I'm Starving* (Yau Ching, 16mm film, 1998)
60: Still from *I'm Starving* (Yau Ching, 16mm film, 1998)
72: Still from *Ho Yuk* (Yau Ching, 35mm film, 2002)
110–111: Still from *We Are Alive* (Yau Ching, digital video, 2010)
114: Still from *We Are Alive* (Yau Ching, digital video, 2010)

Acknowledgments

Grateful acknowledgment is made to the following publications in which these translations first appeared, sometimes in earlier versions.

Arkansas International: "Dissolve Into Wind," "Ethical Reasoning Directed at a Steak"

Asymptote: "A Beautiful Crisis," "I am a Foot," "The Temptations of Eden," "Island Country"

QUEER - A Collection of LGBTQ Writing from Ancient Times to Yesterday (Head of Zeus, 2021, ed. Frank Wynne.): "A Beautiful Crisis," "I am a Foot," "The Temptations of Eden," "Island Country"

Mantis: "Private Furniture Symphony," "No City"

The Margins (AAWW): "Turning a Leaf," "October"

Catamaran Literary Reader: "Notestone"

Two Lines: "Always," "Spacetime"

Words Without Borders and *Academy of American Poets Poem-a-Day*: "Trial Run"

Your Echo Comes Back in Greek: A Festschrift in Honor of Rosanna Warren on the Occasion of her Retirement: "Inside Me," "October," "Spacetime"

I am grateful for having met Chenxin almost ten years ago, first online, then in Hong Kong. Her brilliant recreations have made me laugh through dark wet pandemic evenings. These translations were made possible through a grant from the Hong Kong Arts Development Council. I thank Liza Morales for taking care of my "home," and Dr. Chou Sucheng for keeping me alive. I am indebted to Amie Parry for reading the manuscript through and picking the book's title, and to Jennifer Feeley for her thoughtful blurb. The past few years would not have been bearable without Polly's unfailing care and endless support. And finally, albeit projecting impatience, to dnf's remaining within reach.

Yau Ching, Hong Kong, Summer 2024

Thank you, first and foremost, to Yau Ching for the immense privilege of translating these poems. Thank you to Steve Bradbury for introducing us and for being the best reader any translator or poet could hope for. Thank you to B.T., a hero. Thank you to Ying, Zixin, and Ed.

Chenxin Jiang

Contributor Biographies

Born in Hong Kong, **Yau Ching** received her education in Hong Kong, New York, and London. She has worked as an editor for a film magazine in Hong Kong, a screenwriter for Hong Kong television, a reporter for New York Chinatown newspapers, a translator for transnational corporations, a video instructor for people with HIV in New York, a curator for queer film festivals in Asia, and has taught in Michigan, Hong Kong and London. Her collections of poems in Chinese include *The Impossible Home* (2000), *Big Hairy Egg* (2011), and *Pre-historic Documents* (2021). She currently teaches at the National Central University, Taiwan. More information is available at www.yauching.com.

Chenxin Jiang is a PEN/Heim-winning translator from Italian, German, and Chinese. She was born in Singapore and grew up in Hong Kong. Chenxin's translation of Yau Ching's poem "Trial Run" was a winner of the 2020 Words Without Borders–Academy of American Poets Poems in Translation Contest. She serves on the board of the American Literary Translators Association.

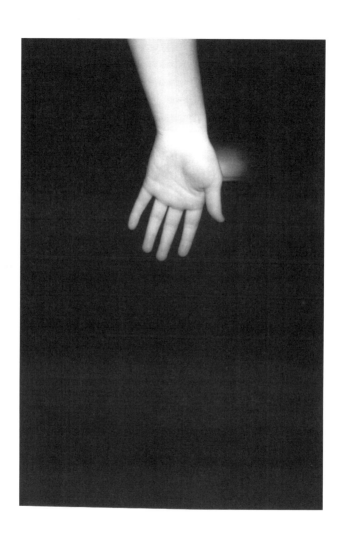